Y0-BCR-081

NO-COOK COOKERY

Ting and Neil Morris

Illustrated by Ruth Levy

SEA-TO-SEA

Mankato Collingwood London

This symbol appears on some pages throughout this book. It indicates that adult supervision is advisable for that activity.

This edition first published in 2007 by
Sea-to-Sea Publications
1980 Lookout Drive
North Mankato
Minnesota 56003

Printed in China

Library of Congress Cataloging-in-Publication Data

Morris, Ting.
   No-cook cookery / by Ting and Neil Morris, authors ; Ruth Levy, illustrator.
      p. cm. -- (Sticky fingers)
   Includes index.
   ISBN-13: 978-1-59771-031-2
   1. Cookery (Cold dishes) I. Morris, Neil, 1946- II. Levy, Ruth. III. Title.

TX830.M67 2006
641.7'9--dc22

2005058176

9 8 7 6 5 4 3 2

Published by arrangement with the Watts Publishing Group Ltd, London

Editor: Hazel Poole
Consultant: Simone Lefolii
Designer: Sally Boothroyd
Photography: John Butcher
Artwork: Ruth Levy
Picture research: Juliet Duff

Contents

Introduction

In this book you can learn something about food both by reading about it and by having fun with simple cooking. The information in the fact boxes will tell you about different foods – where they come from, how they are grown and processed, and their importance in customs and festivals around the world.

We call it "no-cook cooking" because you will not be baking, frying, or using the oven. Instead, you will be having fun measuring, stirring, mixing, rolling, and decorating, with results that look and taste good! Some of the activities involve heating, cutting, and peeling, so please always make sure that an adult is there to help you.

At the end of the book there is information on how food gives us energy, and the importance of a balanced diet. There is also a list of books to read if you want to find out more.

Now you can get ready to get your fingers sticky – following simple recipes and making delicious things to eat, as you read about food.

Equipment and ingredients

The recipes in this book provide an introduction to cooking and need little adult help. Cooking activities that involve using heat or sharp knives are all specially marked. Always read the recipe through before you start, to make sure that you have all the necessary equipment and ingredients. You won't always have to weigh things, as the weight is usually printed on the package that the food comes in. To make things easy, small amounts are given in level tablespoons.

When you are ready to start, put on an apron, wash your hands, and gather together all the equipment and ingredients you will need. If you follow the instructions carefully, the results will be mouthwatering and fun - and when you've finished, don't forget to clean up and put everything away!

In this book the following equipment and ingredients are used:

EQUIPMENT
aluminum foil
baking pan
bowls
brush (for glue)
cake board
candy (strawberry laces; licorice; jelly beans)
candy wrappers
cardboard
cellophane
cereal box (empty)
chocolate box (empty)
colored paper
cupcake cases
cutting board
electric mixer
forks
glass pitcher
grater
ice-cream tub (large)
ice-cube tray
icing bag and nozzle
knife
labels
ladle
mixing bowls
muslin cloth
old magazines
palette knife

paper (colored paper; tissue paper; wrapping paper)
petit-four cases
plastic bag
plastic bowl
plastic wrap
plate
popsicle molds
popsicle sticks
PVA glue
ribbon
rolling pin
saucepan
scissors
screw-top jar
sieve
skewers
small cups
spoons
toothpicks
wax paper
weights
whisk
wire rack
wooden spoon

INGREDIENTS
almond or Heath Bar chips
almond extract
apple juice

baking chocolate
bran
bread (brown; white; dinner rolls; French bread roll; crusty rolls)
carbonated water
cheese (cream cheese; cottage cheese; American cheese)
chocolate sprinkles
cocoa powder
coconut or chocolate coating
concentrated lemon juice
condensed milk
dried apricots
eggs
food colorings
fruit (apples; bananas; lemons; limes; oranges; pawpaw; pineapple; strawberries; tomatoes)
ginger ale
grape juice
grenadine
ground almonds
heavy cream
ice cubes
jam
margarine
milk

mint leaves
nuts (almonds; cashews; hazelnuts)
oats (jumbo and regular)
orange punch
parsley
peanut oil
pound cake
raisins (brown and yellow)
rye flakes
shredded coconut
shredded wheat
soft margarine
soy milk
sugar (brown; white superfine; vanilla; confectioner's)
sugar balls (small sugar candies)
sunflower seeds
Swiss rolls
vanilla extract
vegetables (carrots; celery; cucumber; lettuce)
water
wheat flakes
whole wheat crackers
yogurt

A Healthy Start

Here's how to start your day with a bowl of healthy muesli.

1 Put the oats and flakes in a large mixing bowl. (If you don't have the different types of flakes, use ordinary oatmeal oats to make up the quantities.) Add the brown sugar and sunflower seeds, and the bran.

2 Cut the raisins and apricots into small pieces. Ask an adult to help you chop up the nuts. Put the fruit and nuts into the bowl and mix all the ingredients together.

3 Put the mixed muesli into the jar and screw the lid on tight. Label the jar, adding the date, and store it in a cool place.

4 Serve your muesli with milk, yogurt, or fresh fruit juice.

5 On cold days you could add the milk or juice and heat the muesli up for five minutes. This will make a nice warm start to the day.

Cereals

Cereals are grasses that produce edible grains, which are the seeds of the plant. These grasses include wheat, oats, rice, corn, barley, millet, sorghum, and rye. They are the most important plant foods in the world, and form a major part of most people's diet.

Cereals give us energy as well as protein, fiber, vitamins, and minerals. Oats come originally from central Europe and are the major ingredient in the original Swiss muesli. They are widely grown in Europe and North America because they are suited to more types of different soils and climates than most cereals. Oats are easy to eat and have a rich, creamy flavor. The Swiss-German word *Müsli* comes from *Mus*, meaning mush or purée. This has become a popular breakfast cereal, because the ingredients are less processed than in other packaged cereals. Muesli is also made with wheat flakes – whole grains of wheat that have been flattened between rollers – and bran, which is the outer protective layer of the grain.

When you get near the bottom of the jar, it's time to make another week's supply of muesli. For variety, add your own selection of fruit, nuts, and seeds.

Cheese Boats

1 To sail a fleet of small boats on a sea of lettuce, first split the dinner rolls in half lengthwise. Spread with margarine. To make sails, cut the cheese slices into triangles and push toothpicks through them and into the rolls. You could add buoys by decorating toothpicks with colorful paper triangles and pushing the picks into small tomatoes. Then arrange the boats and buoys on a crunchy lettuce sea.

2 Stay at sea with French bread submarines and a luxury sandwich liner. Mix the cottage cheese and cream cheese together, and beat the mixture until it is smooth and fluffy.

3 Slice the banana and sprinkle it with lemon juice to keep it from turning brown. Then mash it up with a fork. Blend 4 tablespoons of sugar and one teaspoon of vanilla sugar into the basic cheese mixture. Add the banana, finely chopped almonds, and a teaspoon of fresh orange juice.

4 Cut a small French bread roll down the middle lengthwise, and hollow out the two halves. Stuff one half with cheese spread and put the other half on top. Use two hollowed-out crusty rolls filled with spread to go with the big submarine. Wrapped in aluminum foil, these submarines are ideal for taking on picnics.

5 You can use the remaining spread on your luxury liner. Cut the crusts off the sliced brown and white bread. Fill two brown sandwiches and one white sandwich with cheese spread.

6 Cut one brown sandwich into an oblong hull, and keep the cut-off strip for a funnel. Cut the other brown sandwich into triangles, to make the bow and stern of the ship, and place them in position.

7 Cut the white sandwich into four squares, and use three of them to make the upper part of the ship. Cut a funnel from the fourth, and put the white and brown funnels in place.

Now you can launch all your boats and have a cheese feast!

Cheese

It is not known for sure when or where cheese was first made. According to one legend, an Arab merchant tasted some milk that had curdled in a goatskin bag. He liked the taste and a new food was discovered! We do know that Greek and Roman scholars wrote about cheese over 2,000 years ago.

Cheese is made from curdled milk, by separating the curd from the liquid whey. The curd is then pressed in a mold and allowed to ripen. The original milk usually comes from cows, goats, or sheep, but in parts of Asia the milk of camels and water buffalo is also used. France produces the widest range of cheeses in the world, and many villages have their own speciality. Camembert, a famous rich, creamy cheese, comes originally from the village of that name in Normandy. Roquefort is named after a village in southern France. This strong cheese is made from sheep's milk and is matured in local caves.

Coconut Bars

YOU WILL NEED:
- ✔ 8-in (20-cm) square baking pan ✔ wax paper ✔ bowl
- ✔ ribbon ✔ 14 oz (400 g) can condensed milk ✔ 12 oz (350 g) shredded coconut
- ✔ 16 oz (500 g) confectioners' sugar ✔ red food coloring
- ✔ sieve ✔ strawberry laces
- ✔ knife ✔ cellophane ✔ metal spoon ✔ wooden spoon

1 Sift the confectioners' sugar into a bowl, and mix it with the condensed milk. Then stir in the shredded coconut with a wooden spoon. This will take a lot of strength, because the mixture is very stiff!

2 Line the base of a baking pan with wax paper, and dust it with confectioners' sugar. Put half of the mixture into the pan, pressing it down firmly with the back of a spoon.

3 Add a few drops of red food coloring to the rest of the mixture. Put only two or three drops in to start with, kneading the mixture carefully. Then press the pink mixture on top of the white mixture in the pan.

4 Leave the mixture to set for at least 12 hours. Then cut it into eight bars. Put strawberry laces around each bar, and then wrap them in cellophane. Tie the ends with ribbon.

Coconut bars make a delicious snack and will keep for one month in an airtight container.

Coconuts

Coconuts are the fruit of the coconut palm. In the fifteenth century, Portuguese sailors thought the undeveloped buds on the outer husk of this huge nut looked rather like a face. So they called the nut *coco*, Portuguese for "grimace." The husk cushions the inner seed when the coconut falls from the tree. Inside is a layer of thick white "meat," and the hollow center is filled with a watery liquid called coconut milk. This makes a refreshing drink. The coconut palm grows up to 100 feet (30 meters) tall and is crowned with long, feathery leaves. One tree can produce about 50 coconuts each year and the largest coconuts in the world can weigh up to 40 lb (18 kg) each. These are harvested by climbing the tree and cutting off a cluster of nuts, or by gathering fallen nuts on the ground. The Philippines, Indonesia, and Sri Lanka are the world's leading coconut producers.

Caribbean Tub

YOU WILL NEED:
- ✔ large margarine or ice-cream tub
- ✔ 1 small pineapple ✔ 1 orange
- ✔ 1 pawpaw ✔ 1 banana
- ✔ 3 tablespoons cashew nuts
- ✔ nut oil   knife ✔ 1 lime
- ✔ cutting board ✔ teaspoon
- ✔ tablespoon

You will need a sharp knife to prepare the fruit for this tub. Ask an adult to help you.

1 Lay the pineapple on its side and cut off the top and bottom. Then cut the pineapple widthwise into 1-inch (2-cm) slices. Cut the skin off each slice, and remove all the tiny black "eyes," as well as the core in the middle. Then cut the slices into chunks and put them in the tub.

2 With a knife, score the orange into quarters and peel off the skin and pith. Cut the orange flesh into slices, quarter them, and add them to the tub.

3 Cut the pawpaw in half lengthwise. Scoop out the seeds and throw them away. Peel the pawpaw, cut it up into small pieces, and put them in the tub.

4 Peel the banana, brush it with a little lime juice, slice it, and put the slices in the tub.

5 Chop up the cashew nuts and mix them in with the fruit.

Bananas

The banana plant first grew in India and southeast Asia. Arab traders took bananas to Africa. Then Portuguese explorers took roots of the plant, and its African name – *banana* – to the Canary Islands. From there it was taken across the Atlantic to the Caribbean and Central America. In recent years bananas have become very popular, especially in Europe. The big countries of Brazil, India, and China are the world's largest banana producers. But small nations such as the Caribbean islands of St. Lucia and Dominica depend on bananas and coconuts for their survival. Bananas are not easy to trade in because they cannot be stored. They must be harvested while they are still green, shipped to other countries, and then delivered to stores – all within 10 to 20 days so that they are ripe and ready to eat. If you want to know where your bananas come from, look at the small label showing their country of origin.

6 Pour a tablespoon of lime juice and a teaspoon of peanut oil all over the salad. Put the lid on the tub and shake it. Then keep it in the refrigerator until it's needed – your Caribbean fruit salad is perfect for packed lunches and picnics.

Thirst Quenchers

Herbal teas are good for you, and they are very thirst-quenching. Here are a couple of ideas, and all you need for your tea party are a teapot, strainer, spoons, cups and boiling water. Always ask an adult to pour on the boiling water. We've also added a strawberry punch for thirsty friends.

1 Pick a handful of mint leaves, and wash and crush them. Put the mint into a teapot and pour in boiling water. Strain the tea after four minutes, and when it is cool, pour it into a glass pitcher.

2 Add the juice of half a lemon, half an orange, some grated lemon and orange peel, and the sugar. Mix well and then chill.

3 When you are ready to serve the mint tea, add the ginger ale and ice cubes. Put a thin slice of lemon or orange and a sprig of fresh mint into each glass.

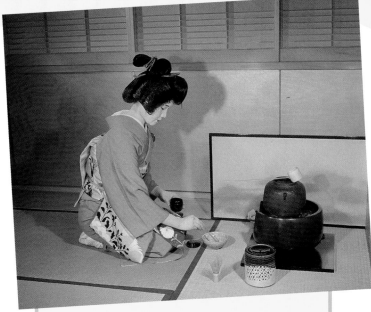

Strawberry punch
YOU WILL NEED:
- ✔ large bowl ✔ 3¹/₂ oz (150 g) sugar
- ✔ 16 oz (500 g) strawberries (fresh or frozen) ✔ ladle ✔ ice cubes
- ✔ 100 ml apple juice ✔ 1 large lemon
- ✔ 500 ml carbonated water
- ✔ 250 ml grape juice

1 Wash the strawberries, put them in a large bowl, add the sugar and the apple juice. Cover the bowl and leave it at room temperature for a couple of hours.

2 Shortly before serving, add the grape juice and lemon juice. Stir and add the carbonated water. Ladle the punch into glasses, add ice cubes, a twist of lemon peel, and a sprig of strawberry leaves.

Japanese tea
According to an ancient legend, tea was discovered by a Chinese emperor around 2700 B.C. Leaves from a wild tea bush fell into his pot of boiling water, and the emperor liked the taste of the new brew. Today, the best tea comes from the mountain slopes of countries with lots of sun and rain. The tea bushes grow slowly and give more flavor. India and China produce most of the world's tea. Much of this is black tea, so called because the leaves turn black after being dried in ovens. The Japanese prefer green tea, made from leaves that are steamed and dried quickly. This tea is light green and has a delicate flavor. In Japan there is an ancient custom of entertaining friends in a formal tea ceremony. The hostess makes the tea according to traditional rules. The guest eats a sweet pastry, sips the fragrant tea, and admires the beauty of the cup. Many Japanese girls are still taught how to perform this beautiful ceremony properly.

15

Halloween Horrors

To make horror faces for a haunting Halloween, ice your own fiendishly mouthwatering cakes.

1 Put the cookies in a plastic bag. Close the bag, and crush the cookies with a rolling pin.

YOU WILL NEED:

Cake Mixture
- ✔ 8 oz (225 g) Zwieback cookies
- ✔ 5 oz (150 g) superfine sugar
- ✔ 4 tablespoons ground almonds
- ✔ 1 or 2 tablespoons milk
- ✔ 2 tablespoons cocoa powder
- ✔ plastic bowl
- ✔ plastic bag
- ✔ rolling pin
- ✔ 2 1/2 oz (75 g) butter (or margarine)

Butter Icing
- ✔ 4 oz (100 g) margarine
- ✔ 8 oz (250 g) confectioners' sugar
- ✔ wooden spoon
- ✔ blue, green, and red food coloring
- ✔ bowls
- ✔ metal spoon

To decorate
- ✔ licorice candies and strips
- ✔ small candies
- ✔ strawberry laces

2 Pour the cookie crumbs into a bowl and mix them with the sugar, cocoa powder, and ground almonds.

3 Soften the butter and pour it into the mixture. Add a little milk, so that the mixture is smooth but firm enough to shape. Divide the mixture into ten pieces, form them into balls, and then flatten them into 1-inch (3-cm) thick round cakes. Let them set in the refrigerator while you prepare the butter icing.

4 Put the margarine in a bowl and beat it with a wooden spoon until it is soft. Sift the confectioners' sugar and add it in small amounts, beating well until the mixture is smooth. Divide it into three small bowls and add a few drops of different food coloring to each bowl. Use a metal spoon to mix in the color, because a wooden spoon will stain.

5 Using the palette knife, cover the top of each cake with blue, green, or red icing. Dip the knife in a mug of warm water when you are smoothing the icing, but leave the red icing rather rough.

6 Decorate your horrors with candies, licorice strips, and strawberry laces. Press them into the icing for a really ghostly look.

Apple horrors

YOU WILL NEED:
- ✔ 4 apples
- ✔ 4 wooden skewers
- ✔ 3¹/₂ oz (100 g) margarine
- ✔ 5 oz (150 g) confectioners' sugar
- ✔ jelly beans
- ✔ blue food coloring
- ✔ licorice candy and strips

1 Wash and dry the apples before pushing a wooden skewer through each one.

3 Dip the apples into the bowl to coat them with icing. Then give your apple horrors jelly bean hair, a candy nose, and a licorice ghoulish grin. Let them set in the refrigerator, and stand them in jelly jars for serving.

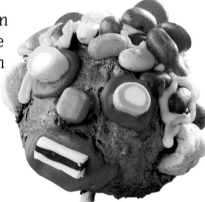

2 Soften the margarine in a large bowl and add sifted confectioners' sugar. When the mixture is smooth, mix in a few drops of blue food coloring.

Halloween customs

The Halloween festival on October 31 probably comes from an ancient Celtic New Year festival. The Celts lived over 2,000 years ago in Britain, Ireland, and northern France. On the last day of the old year the Druids, who were the priests and teachers of the Celts, lit huge bonfires to drive away evil spirits. To protect themselves further, the Druids offered the spirits good things to eat.

The autumn leaves, corn, apples, and nuts that have become such a part of the Halloween season are reminders of the Druids' festival to celebrate harvest time. Today bobbing for apples is a favorite Halloween game. A large bowl is filled with water and apples are put in. The object of the game is to try and catch an apple in your mouth and take it out of the bowl, without using your hands. This sounds quite easy, but just try it!

Bird's Nests

Here's how to make some birds and eggs to put in their nest. Make the birds and eggs a day before the nests, as they take about 24 hours to harden.

YOU WILL NEED:
- ✔ 2 tablespoons butter ✔ 1 tablespoon milk ✔ spoon
- ✔ juice and grated rind of 1 lemon ✔ 16 oz (450 g) confectioners' sugar ✔ blue and yellow food coloring
- ✔ sugar balls ✔ bird-shaped cookie cutter (optional)
- ✔ rolling pin ✔ saucepan ✔ 2 bowls ✔ scissors
- ✔ 12 cupcake cases ✔ 8 oz (200 g) baking chocolate
- ✔ 1 tablespoon soft margarine ✔ piece of cardboard
- ✔ 2 oz (60 g) shredded wheat ✔ water ✔ plastic wrap

1 Melt and gently heat the butter, milk, grated lemon rind, and two tablespoons of lemon juice in a pan. Do not boil.

2 When the mixture is cool, slowly add the confectioners' sugar. If the mixture is too dry, add a few more drops of lemon juice.

3 Dust your work surface with confectioners' sugar, and knead the mixture until it is a smooth, pliable dough.

4 Divide the mixture into two bowls and knead a few drops of food coloring into each mixture – blue in one, yellow in the other. If the mixture gets too moist, work in a little more confectioners' sugar.

5 Cut out the birds with a bird-shaped cutter, or use this stencil. Copy the bird shape onto a piece of cardboard 2 x 1 1/2 in (5 x 4 cm) and cut it out. Roll out the blue icing to a thickness of 1/4 in (5 mm). Put the stencil on the icing and cut around it with a knife. Cut out four birds, adding a sugar ball for the birds' eyes. Use the rest of the blue icing to make sugar eggs. Keep the dough wrapped in plastic wrap.

6 Make some yellow birds and eggs in the same way, and then leave them to harden at room temperature.

7 Melt the chocolate and margarine in a bowl by placing this over a small saucepan of hot water. Ask an adult to help.

8 Break the shredded wheat into small pieces and stir them in.

9 Spoon the mixture into the cupcake cases. Decorate each nest with one of your birds and some eggs. Leave to set.

Why not make some of these bird's nests next Easter?

Wheat

People first grew wheat many thousands of years ago in the Middle East. In ancient Egypt, Greece, and Rome, grain became such an important part of life that it was often used to pay taxes. Later wheat was grown all over Europe, and Spanish conquerors took it to Mexico in the 1520s. By the early seventeenth century, English settlers were growing wheat in America. Today, the greatest producers of wheat are China, the former Soviet Union, and the United States. It is fairly easy to grow wheat, which is usually planted with a machine called a seed drill. When the wheat is ripe, it is cut and separated using a combine harvester. There are many varieties of wheat, and two main types – common and durum wheat. Common, or bread, wheat is mainly grown to be milled into flour for baking. It is also used for breakfast cereals. Shredded wheat is made from toasted whole wheat. Durum wheat grows well in dry conditions and is used to make semolina and pasta such as spaghetti.

The Big Chill

You don't need an ice-cream maker to make these fabulous frozen treats.

1 Wash and hull the strawberries. Then put them in a large bowl, sprinkle on the confectioners' sugar, and mash them with a fork into a smooth pulp.

Strawberry scoop
YOU WILL NEED:
- ✔ silver foil ✔ 16 oz (500 g) strawberries ✔ electric mixer ✔ mixing bowl
- ✔ fork ✔ 1 tablespoon confectioners' sugar
- ✔ 2½ oz (75 g) sugar
- ✔ 300 ml heavy cream
- ✔ 4 oz (125 g) plain yogurt
- ✔ large bowl ✔ popsicle sticks ✔ plastic container
- ✔ small cups

2 Ask an adult to help you beat the cream in a bowl until it is thick. Add the sugar and beat until the cream forms stiff peaks.

3 Add the cream to the strawberry pulp, and put the mixture in a plastic container, covering it with silver foil. Put it in the freezer for an hour.

4 After an hour, beat the mixture with a fork to break up any ice crystals. Put it back in the freezer and do the same thing again an hour later. Strawberry ice cream takes up to three hours to freeze properly.

5 Cool off with a frozen yogurt feast. Mix a tablespoon of the strawberry pulp with a teaspoon of sugar and the yogurt. Fill small cups with the mixture and cover them with aluminum foil. Push popsicle sticks through the foil tops before putting them in the freezer.

Popsicle galore

YOU WILL NEED:
- ✔ 4 popsicle molds and sticks
- ✔ 150 ml orange punch
- ✔ 100 ml grenadine
- ✔ ice-cube tray   ✔ 1 lemon
- ✔ strawberries or other fruit (apple, peach, kiwi)
- ✔ water   ✔ plastic wrap
- ✔ toothpicks

1 Push the popsicle sticks halfway into the molds. Pour 150 ml (a glass) of orange punch into a pitcher and add a squeeze of lemon. Make up another pitcher with 100 ml of grenadine diluted with 50 ml of water. Half fill the molds with orange or strawberry and put them in the freezer for an hour.

2 Cut two strawberries (or other fruit) into thin slices. Take the popsicles out of the freezer, and arrange the fruit slices in the molds, leaving enough space to cover the fruit with the rest of the juice. Put the molds back in the freezer. After about an hour your popsicles will be ready to eat. Hold them under running water to remove them from the molds.

3 For an extra treat, make some mini popsicles. You can use any fruit juice or cola drink. Just fill the sections of an ice-cube tray with the drink and cover it with plastic wrap. Push a toothpick or popsicle stick through the plastic into each section, and freeze for two hours.

History of ice cream

Ice cream may have first been made in China almost 5,000 years ago. It is said that 3,000 years later the Roman Emperor Nero sent slaves to the mountains to bring back snow, which was then served with honey and fruit. The explorer Marco Polo supposedly tasted flavored ices on his travels through Asia, and took the recipes back to Italy in 1295. There are certainly references in books to ices being sold on the streets of Naples by 1690. A New York newspaper advertised an ice-cream "tavern" in 1786, when it was still a very special dish. The ice-cream cone was invented at an American exhibition in 1904. One story is that when an ice-cream vendor ran out of clean dishes, the person in the next booth gave him a waffle rolled into the shape of a cone. Ice cream was quickly put into it and the ice-cream cone was born!

Chocolate Surprise

MESSY ACTIVITY

YOU WILL NEED:
✔ 3 1/2 oz (100 g) ground almonds
✔ 1 teaspoon jam   ✔ 2 Swiss rolls
✔ 1 egg   ✔ 2 tablespoons cocoa powder
✔ 1 teaspoon each vanilla and almond
   extract   ✔ chocolate sprinkles   ✔ milk
✔ almond or Heath Bar chips   ✔ spoon
✔ coconut or chocolate coating
✔ 20 petit-four cases   ✔ large bowl
✔ 3 saucers   ✔ candy wrappers   ✔ brush
✔ empty chocolate box   ✔ PVA glue
✔ ribbon   ✔ empty cereal box   ✔ water
✔ wrapping and tissue paper   ✔ scissors
✔ old magazines

1 Crumble the Swiss rolls into a large bowl. Add the almonds, jam, cocoa powder, and extracts.

2 Separate the egg and add the yolk to the mixture. Keep the egg white in a separate bowl – you will need it later. Mix all the ingredients until the mixture is smooth and creamy. Add a drop of milk if it is too dry.

3 Divide the mixture into about twenty portions, and roll them into small balls.

4 Put the chocolate sprinkles, almond chips, and coconut coating into separate saucers. Dip the balls first in egg white, then in one of the three coatings, and place them in petit-four cases.

5 To gift-wrap your truffles, stick candy wrappers or magazine cut-outs onto an empty chocolate box. Cover the whole box and then varnish it with PVA glue diluted with a little water. Make sure the box is completely dry before filling it with chocolate truffles and tying it with ribbon.

6 Or you could make a basket for your truffles. Coat an empty cereal box with glue, and then cover it with wrapping paper. Draw a zigzag line all around the box, leaving 1 1/2 inches (4 cm) on each side for the handle. Cut away the shaded part, overlap the two handle strips, and glue them together. Put tissue paper at the bottom of the basket and put the truffles in. They are so delicious, they won't stay there long!

Chocolate

When the Spanish conqueror Hernan Cortes defeated the Aztecs in 1521, he found the Mexican Indians using cacao beans to make a drink. They called this *xocolatl*, and it was the favorite drink of the Aztec emperor, Montezuma. Cortes took cacao beans back to Spain, where chocolate became the special drink of rich aristocrats. The Spaniards sweetened it with sugar and tried adding new flavors, such as cinnamon and other spices. Three hundred years later a Dutchman named Van Houten invented a press that squeezed the rich cocoa butter out of cacao beans. This was then molded into bars, and people began to eat chocolate as well as drink it. It was still coarse and bitter, but in 1876 a Swiss manufacturer put milk into his chocolate and produced a new flavor. Further refinements have produced the smooth, velvety chocolate we know today. But it still all begins with the seeds of the cacao tree.

Express Cake

To catch this cake, ...

YOU WILL NEED:
- ✔ 16 oz (450 g) pound cake   ✔ 2 eggs
- ✔ 20 oz (600 g) confectioners' sugar
- ✔ chocolate Swiss roll   ✔ red, yellow, black and green food coloring   ✔ 4 tablespoons butter icing bag (or wax paper) and small nozzle   ✔ licorice candies and wheels
- ✔ candies   ✔ knife   ✔ wire rack   ✔ bowls
- ✔ whisk   ✔ tablespoon   ✔ palette knife
- ✔ sieve   ✔ cake board   ✔ wooden spoon

1 Cut a 1-inch (2 cm) thick slice from the base of the pound cake and place it on a wire rack to form the base for the locomotive boiler. Cut the rest of the cake in two widthwise, as shown.

2 Stand the larger piece upright behind the base, for the cab, and the smaller piece behind the cab, to form the tender.

3 Now make some red icing to coat the cake. Crack the eggs and separate the whites from the yolks. Beat the egg whites in a bowl until frothy. Sift 14 oz (400 g) confectioners' sugar and whisk it into the egg white a tablespoon at a time. Beat for about 10 minutes until the icing is soft and forms peaks. Then add some red food coloring drop by drop. You might have to add more sugar if it gets too sticky.

4 Use a palette knife to spread on the icing. Coat the top and sides of the base, cab, and tender, and let them set for at least eight hours.

5 When the icing is hard, put the three pieces together on a board. Then put the Swiss roll on top of the base to form the boiler. Now you can join and decorate the locomotive with butter icing.

6 Beat the butter with a wooden spoon until it is soft. Add 6 oz (150 g) sifted confectioners' sugar in small amounts. Divide the mixture into small bowls and add different coloring to each one.

7 Using a small nozzle in an icing bag, decorate the edges of the locomotive, covering up the seams as you go. Write a number on the cab.

8 If you don't want to make your own icing, you can use instant sugar paste. The piping tubes have different colors and are ideal for express decorators.

9 Add some licorice wheels, a chimney, and a window, and put candies on top of the tender.

European cakes

Roman honey cake and medieval sweet cakes were the sponge and iced cakes of today. Some cake recipes have been around for thousands of years. The ancient Romans created cheesecake, using a cheese similar to the Italian ricotta we know today – a soft white cheese made from sheep's milk. Today cheesecake can be found on restaurant menus and supermarket shelves around the world. During the 1800s, cakes became real creations. The French and Austrians made such wonderful desserts that people traveled to Paris and Vienna just to taste them. The Sachertorte is named after a famous Viennese hotel manager of the nineteenth century. This rich chocolate cake is almost the national dish of Austria. In France the traditional Christmas cake is a chocolate log, while in Italy it is the panettone –a light, spiced, breadlike cake. Cakes are made from similar recipes around the world, but local variations make them all the more interesting to taste!

Now hurry to catch the express before it's gone!

Tofu Spread

1 First make some tofu in your own press. Put a sieve over a mixing bowl and line it with a clean piece of cloth – muslin is best. Find a plate that fits into the sieve to act as a lid, and three or four weights.

YOU WILL NEED:
- ✔ metal sieve ✔ mixing bowl ✔ muslin cloth ✔ plate
- ✔ weights ✔ 2 tablespoons concentrated lemon juice
- ✔ warm water ✔ 250 ml soy milk ✔ small saucepan
- ✔ ladle ✔ 1 carrot ✔ celery ✔ cucumber ✔ parsley
- ✔ grater ✔ spoon

2 Mix the concentrated lemon juice with 2 oz (50 ml) of warm water.

3 Ask an adult to help you heat the soy milk in a small saucepan. Remove it from the heat just before it boils.

4 Quickly stir the milk, and while it is swirling around, drip half the lemon mixture into it over the back of a spoon. Try to cover the whole surface of the milk.

5 Slowly stir the milk five times all around the saucepan, touching the bottom and sides with your spoon. Cover the saucepan and leave it to cool for three minutes.

6 Trickle the remaining lemon mixture over the back of a spoon into the center and outer edges of the milk. The milk will now start to curdle. Gently stir it three or four times around the sides and the surface. Then cover the saucepan and leave for another six minutes.

7 When you uncover the milk, you will find that it has curdled. The white parts are the curds, and the yellow fluid is whey. To squeeze the whey from the curds, ladle the curdled milk into the cloth-lined sieve in your tofu press. Wrap the cloth over the mixture and put the lid and the weights on top. Leave for 40 minutes.

8 Then press the lid down firmly to make sure all the whey has been pressed out. You will be left with a lump of tofu, which you can shape into a bar and keep in a bowl of cold water in the refrigerator for up to a week. Change the water daily.

9 Now you can make a delicious tofu spread. Grate the carrot, celery, and some cucumber, and add a tablespoon of chopped parsley. Mix all the ingredients into the tofu and blend it into a smooth spread.

Soy beans

Soy beans have been grown in China and Japan for thousands of years. The soy bean plant grows to about three feet (one meter) in height. It produces pods, each of which usually contains two or three beans, or seeds. Soy beans are highly nutritious. Because they contain so much protein, many East Asian people use them in the way that meat and eggs are used in Western countries. In East Asia people eat soy paste, sauce, milk, cheese, sprouts, and curd. Tofu is the Japanese word for soybean curd, which is made from soy milk. Soy beans are pulped, heated, and sieved to extract soy milk. In the East, tofu shops are as common as bakeries in the West. Tofu makers rise at dawn to prepare fresh produce daily. Some families eat tofu three times a day. In recent years it has caught on in Europe and America among health food eaters and lovers of Oriental food. And now you can make your own!

Food for Energy

All living things need energy to stay alive. For human beings that energy comes from the food we eat. Our bodies need nutrients for growth as well as for energy. There are several groups of nutrients

Carbohydrates
These are an important source of energy and include sugars and starches. Bread, potatoes, pasta, and rice contain a lot of carbohydrate.

Proteins
These are essential to build and maintain healthy bones, muscles, and skin; to ensure chemical reactions take place and to help protect against disease. Good sources include meat, fish, eggs, nuts, beans, and cheese.

Fats
Fats are full of energy and carry important vitamins, but eating too many fatty foods is unhealthy. Fats are found in meat, dairy products, and nuts.

Minerals
We need only small amounts of minerals each day, for growth and maintenance and to take part in chemical reactions in the body. Two important minerals are calcium and iron. Calcium is found in milk and whole-wheat bread, and iron in meat and eggs.

Bread and cereals
Bread, cereals, corn, pasta, potatoes.

Dairy products
Milk, cheese, yogurt.

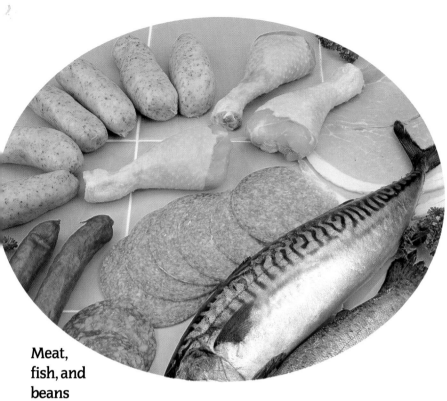

**Meat,
fish, and
beans**
Red meat, fish, beans, poultry, eggs, nuts.

**Vegetables
and fruit**
Vegetables, fruit.

Vitamins
These are needed by body cells and to regulate body processes. Vitamin C, for example, is used in many processes and is found in citrus fruits and some vegetables.

Fiber
Fiber helps other foods pass easily through the digestive system. Good sources are whole wheat bread, brown rice, and wholegrain pasta, as well as beans, vegetables, and fruit.

Water
The body uses water in several ways. It is part of the blood, it helps keep our bodies cool when we sweat, and it carries wastes out of the body in urine. Water is present in other liquids and in various amounts in solid foods.

Healthy eating
Most foods contain several nutrients. Bread, for example, is rich in carbohydrates, protein, and some minerals. Foods that are rich in nutrients can be grouped together in four basic food groups. It is important for good health to have a balanced diet by eating a variety of foods from all these groups.

Glossary

Aztecs - Mexican Indians whose empire was destroyed by Spanish conquerors in the early sixteenth century.

blend - to mix together thoroughly.

bran - the outer protective layer of a grain.

cacao - a tropical tree whose seeds are used to make cocoa and chocolate.

cereals - grasses that produce edible grains.

cinnamon - a spice obtained from the bark of the cinnamon tree.

combine harvester - a machine that cuts, threshes, and cleans cereals such as wheat.

curd - a semisolid substance formed by adding acid to milk.

curdle - to turn into curd.

dessert - a sweet course at the end of a meal.

diet - the food and drink that a person regularly has.

dilute - to make weaker by adding water.

fiber - a substance that helps other foods pass easily through the body's digestive system.

grain - the seed of a cereal plant.

grate - to rub (on a grater) to make into small shreds.

Halloween - a festival on October 31, the eve of All Saints' Day.

hull - to remove the outer covering of a fruit.

ingredient - an item of food listed in a recipe.

knead - to work and press into a mixture with your hands.

minerals - substances in food that are needed for growth and maintenance of the body and to take part in chemical reactions in the body.

muesli - a mixture of oats, nuts, and fruit eaten with milk.

muslin - a fine cotton fabric.

nutrient - a substance that gives life and growth.

nutritious - nourishing, giving life and growth.

petit four - a small, sweet cake.

pith - the tissue lining the inside of the rind of fruit.

protein - substances that are essential for building and maintaining the body, for chemical reactions, and to protect against disease.

punch - a mixed drink containing fruit juice.

rind - the outer layer of a fruit, cheese, or bacon.

score - to make cuts in.

seed drill - a machine for planting seeds.

skewer - a long "pin" for holding food in position.

tofu - soybean curd, made from soy milk.

vanilla - a flavoring extract from the pods of the vanilla plant.

Resources

vitamins - substances in food that are needed by body cells and for body processes.

whey - watery liquid that separates from curd when milk curdles.

Books to read

The Lunch Book and Bag: A Fit Kid's Guide to Making Delicious (& Nutritious) Lunches
by Jolene Bodily and Kinny Kreisworth
(Toronto: Somerville House Books, 1998)

Betty Crocker's Kids Cook!
by Betty Crocker
(New York: Betty Crocker, 1999)

Emeril's There's a Chef in My Family!: Recipes to Get Everybody Cooking
by Emeril Lagasse
(New York: HarperCollins: 2004)

The Kid's Cookbook: A Great Book for Kids Who Love to Cook!
by Abigail Johnson Dodge
(Birmingham, AL: Oxmoor House: 2000)

The Nancy Drew Cookbook: Clues to Good Cooking
by Carolyn G. Keene
(New York: Grosset & Dunlap, 2005)

The Usborne Little Round The World Cookbook: Internet Linked
by Angela Wilkes, Fiona Watt
(New York: Usborne Books, 2004)

Websites

Betty Crocker
www.bettycrocker.com

The Boston Cooking-School Cookbook
www.bartleby.com/87/

Kids Cooking Corner
www.kidscookingcorner.com

Veggie Kids
http://my.execpc.com/~veggie/tips.html

Index

Additional Photographs:
Zefa Picture Library 9, 13, 15, 17, 19, 20, 23, 27, cover; Robert Harding 7, 11, 25